KYLIE
FASHION

KYLIE FASHION

KYLIE MINOGUE & WILLIAM BAKER

FOREWORD BY JEAN PAUL GAULTIER

With 346 illustrations, 269 in colour

Thames & Hudson

CONTENTS

JEAN PAUL GAULTIER

Dear Kylie

Do you remember the first time we met? It was in the early 1990s, for the opening of my first boutique in London. Stéphane Sednaoui – model, muse, fashion photographer, music video filmmaker and friend to us both – introduced me to you. I was struck by your beauty, your kindness, your *joie de vivre*, your charming and unique personality. That was the beginning of a long friendship.

I've been a fan of your music since you arrived in Europe, and have always followed your career and appreciated the big metamorphoses you've gone through: from the little 'So Lucky' ingénue and the so-eighties 'Especially For You' (with Jason) to many memorable moments in terms of images and fashion. Who could forget the gold hot pants and the white jumpsuit with the openings so deep that anyone could feel your pale, delicate skin? You are like a chameleon. You change, you transform yourself, you adapt with the evolution of times, fashions and desires...and still you always stay yourself: our Kylie! This quality is the privilege of '*Les Grandes*'.

When I had the opportunity to work with you and William Baker on your costumes for the world tour in 2007, I was very excited and enjoyed it so much. You knew what you wanted and what you didn't. You were extremely precise and professional. You were always kind, happy and positive, with never a bad thought on your mind. Haute couture fittings are long and you would stand still for hours, very beautiful and always smiling, very much concentrating on 'the action'... I realized that you have, most of all, courage to surmount any difficulty.

You love fashion, and fashion loves you too!

With this book, everyone will realize how strong your influence has been on images (with fab photographers), on clothes (with great designers), and on style.

Kylie, *chérie*, another point I have in common with you: your absolute eye and taste for goodlooking men. You choose them as well as you choose your dresses. Congratulations!

À très bientot, Kylie, *chérie*,

Humanly and fashionably yours,

Post scriptum: I saw Leos Carax's movie, *Holy Motors*, at the Cannes film festival: very good choice on your part...and you are a fabulous actress.

WILLIAM BAKER

It is difficult to believe that it is 25 years since Kylie Ann Minogue released her first single, 'Locomotion', in the wake of her success in Australian soap opera *Neighbours*. There is no doubt that the soap provided a solid foundation for her musical career. By the time 'I Should Be So Lucky' was released in the UK, Kylie was a household name and the single went straight to Number One.

Her musical career is still going strong, and her silver pop anniversary is the perfect opportunity for celebration. Longevity in the music industry is rare; only a few manage to overcome the fickle tastes of the audience. Kylie's ever-changing image and style, as expressed in photo shoots, magazine covers, music videos and on stage, have been key ingredients. She is a dynamic work in progress. As with her music, she works hard to keep it fresh, to try new things. Like most girls, she also loves clothes.

Fashion and pop music have always been a particularly intoxicating cocktail. Certain artists are as famous for a look as they are for their extensive music catalogues. Elvis Presley's quiff, the Beatles' suits and bowl cuts, Madonna's conical bras, Michael Jackson's crystal glove... It's amusing that when people think of Kylie, a pair of gleaming gold hot pants immediately come to mind. In fact, when working on this book, at one point we realized that we had forgotten to include the infamous hot pants. For us they are just a tiny, glittering part of a much bigger picture!

I met Kylie in 1994. By then she had firmly established herself as a fashion icon, having graced the covers of UK style bibles *The Face* and *i-D*, and there was a keen anticipation of what she would do next, having severed her ties with producers Stock, Aitken and Waterman. It was a particularly exciting time in fashion. The pages of Italian *Vogue* and the catwalks of London, Paris and New York were graced by the supermodels at the apex of their glamour. The incredible powerhouse that is Madonna had also become part of the cultural landscape, creating some of the most enduring and inspiring fusions of fashion and pop that have ever been seen. It all provided rich and exciting terrain in which Kylie could learn.

Her nights were spent in West London clubs; her days were spent in Paris, shopping and educating herself about fashion and its influences. She wore the hippest designers of the time – Azzedine Alaïa, John Galliano, Vivienne Westwood, Martin Margiela and Véronique Leroy. She was also consolidating her teams behind the scenes to ensure the best possible visual results. Her fashion prowess has been refined over the years by countless talented individuals, most of whom feature in the pages of this book. As with any creative artist, her work evolves and changes as *she* evolves and changes, often as the result of those around her.

Kylie is a naturally generous person and performer. She simply gives – whether it is to her fans, an audience, a photographer, her friends or collaborators. She possesses a tremendous warmth of spirit and expects nothing except that she is getting the best in return. She presents herself willingly as a blank canvas for experimentation and creative inspiration. She is also full of ideas herself, and has a very natural and real chic, but she loves being 'the subject' and has the wisdom and grace to allow people around her freedom of expression, as she is fully aware that freedom brings out the best in others. She pushes those around her, often out of their own comfort zones, and sees things in others that they often can't see themselves. I began as her stylist and morphed into her creative partner and director, live show director and now photographer.

I have always seen Kylie as an icon and that has been the driving creative force behind my work with her. I studied theology at university because I was fascinated and seduced by the power and evocative allure of language and imagery. True icons hint at something beyond the tangible, possessing a resonance far deeper than their surface layer. I wanted to display Kylie to the world as a gleaming, glittering icon, seducing her audience with her charm and grace through performance and imagery.

Looking through the images in this book brings back truly happy memories of a friendship and a career that I feel incredibly blessed to have, as well as a visual record of our favourite style moments. As deliberate and planned as many of our endeavours have been, we owe just as much to an organic serendipity and a creative symbiosis. I hope our memories bring a smile to your face, too. Kylie, after all, is about good times and celebrating those good times. Kylie is, quite simply, joy.

above

KYLIE

My first music video was a big moment for me. Fashion-wise it was all about fun accessible high street clothing. Fashion houses and haute couture were not on my radar at all back then. But I did love fashion, and revelled in the opportunity to dress up.

opposite

STEPHEN JONES

I was always a fan of Kylie's, and also the hat from her debut album cover. I never imagined one day I would meet her.

MRS JONES

The first time I was aware of Kylie was around the time of *Neighbours*. I had the same hat as her – that large-brimmed sunhat that you pile your 1980s pineapple hair through!

KYLIE

When I was younger, I wasn't used to being photographed in a fashion sense. As a character through acting, sure, but this new set of photographic requirements took me years and years to get used to. Some photographers were great, very helpful and understanding. Others were only used to photographing models and would try to get me to do what models do. Clearly I am not a model build. This would really irritate and sometimes upset me, as I felt like I couldn't be myself. Over time I found what worked for me.

NICOLE BONYTHON

We met in Kylie's songstress infancy so she really hadn't worked herself out yet, and I was very opinionated and had a fairly clear idea of how I thought she should dress. I was used to working with models, so she was challenging to me in that I was used to working with height, but she was perfectly in proportion. She was incredibly open to my suggestions and really game, which was great. I felt that we very much worked together. I don't think any decision was made without her absolute input and oft times it was driven by her.

PETER MORRISSEY

As a fashion designer, it was a huge turning point in my career having Kylie believe in me and support my art through her own. She is a beautiful example of a successful businesswoman and gentlewoman. She was amazing to work with because – no matter what it was concerning in regards to her career, her look and her style – she was always involved. She had a voice, an opinion and a great fashion sense that matched her fame.

previous pages & overleaf

SIMON FOWLER

When Kylie bounced into my studio for the first time in 1989, with no make-up, jeans and a woolly hat, she had a very big smile and said 'Hi, mate.' For one split second I didn't recognize her! All in all I photographed her four or five times. I knew the sessions would produce great shots because she had this ability to try out new things without a care or worry. There's a synergy that happens between her and the camera that makes the end result come alive. Very few people possess this talent, but she does in abundance, and she can make any fashion piece look good. Kylie rocks!

opposite

KYLIE

In the beginning, I guess I just tried out everything. I was game, eager to please and wanted the best end result. I had to find my style on the public stage. Naturally this made for plenty of mishaps, either by myself or by misguidance, but it was the only way to learn.

right

KYLIE

By now I was pretty much based in London and the fashion scene there was my biggest influence. Shops like The Garage on King's Road and Portobello market were regular haunts. I started meeting designers, photographers, directors and artists, both on and off duty. It was all very intoxicating, fun and inspiring.

SF 518-15

SF 619-10

SF 617 *24

opposite

PETER MORRISSEY

Often celebrities are safe and boring, in that they wear a designer outfit only to 'dress to impress'. Kylie would 'dress to express'. It was about who she was and where she was at in life at that exact moment, so it was unique. It was 'Kylie Style'.

KYLIE

At one of my first live concerts, this Morrissey Edmiston two-piece was worn under a crème suit. On stage I whipped off the suit, held in place with good old-fashioned Velcro. Hah, the classic! I'm very moved by these kinds of photographs, as they remind me of how it was in the very beginning.

above

KYLIE

My first shoot for *Vogue* felt so 'grown up'. We shot at the legendary Raymond's Revue Bar in Soho and I was mainly wearing Thierry Mugler and Christian Lacroix. I loved the drama and excess of the styling, and it's interesting to see that this was the first time I was portrayed as a showgirl. A sign of things to come!

above
KYLIE
Filming the 'Step Back in Time' video meant
lots of OTT pieces and I loved all of it. The
Mary Quant Lurex tights/bodysuit made many
appearances around that time. Vintage clothing
has always been a major part of my wardrobe.
As a teenager, I scoured the local markets for
vintage finds.

above

NICOLE BONYTHON

This was an era when fashion was really changing and becoming more interesting and youthful. Kylie and fashion met at the same point. It was like she was the right person, right body, right product, right fashion moment, and there was a wonderful serendipity. I think that together we started a ball rolling that she continued and developed and expanded upon.

KYLIE

Nicole educated me on the true basics of fashion. I learnt so much from her. Our most memorable fashion moment has to be the video for 'Better the Devil You Know'. Nicole bought the material for the plastic mac at a hardware store and had it made. Teamed with hot pants, a bra and Dinosaur Designs jewelry, it became a citable look; also the teeny black dress I jumped around in. It was such an exciting time.

WILLIAM
Some of my personal favourite imagery that Kylie
has produced depicts what the media christened
'Sex Kylie', gyrating in full throttle!

KYLIE
Michael Hutchence was with me on this shoot in the
United States. He loved watching me grow into a
young woman. I loved shooting outdoors, and to this
day prefer to be in a 'real' environment than in a studio.

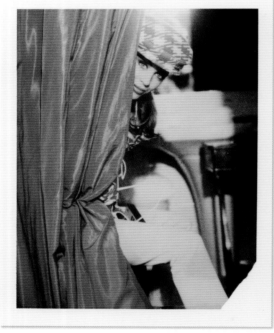

DAVID THOMAS

This shoot with photographer Ellen von Unwerth took place at a grand old hotel off the Champs-Elysées in Paris. Back then it wasn't easy to borrow fashion samples for celebrities (fashion houses favoured editorial shoots with models), but Kylie was an exception. She was fast becoming a favourite of the fashion world, with her perfect sample-size figure and fun, sexy image. When we arrived in Paris, Kylie and I visited Azzedine Alaïa in his space on rue de la Verrerie in the Marais district. The normally shy designer instantly took a liking to Kylie, cooking us lunch in his small apartment above the studio. He chatted away in French, his PR girl interpreting what he was saying. 'I can speak English, but the only person I will speak it to is the Queen Mother,' he exclaimed. For this shoot he allowed us to take whatever we wanted from his Spring 1991 collection, in my view one of his finest.

i·D

i-D MAGAZINE
i-DEAS, FASHION, CLUBS, MUSIC, PEOPLE

LOVE life!

fetish holidays,
lover's fashion and
the dating game

hard workwear
liverpool's new merseybeat
dance dissident gary clail
feminist porn

kylie minogue
on love, life
and manipulation

9 770262 357006

03

USA $5.50

FRANCS 33 LIRE 6,500 DM 12.50 PESETAS 685 0 KR 49

DAVID THOMAS

This cover marks one of my favourite sessions. Judy Blame was art directing, and it was my first shoot with Robert Erdmann. The PVC corset was from Rigby & Peller and the striped chiffon dress was by Betty Jackson. My most vivid memory is of Kylie armed with a pair of scissors, reviewing contact sheets of a previous shoot of hers. She was cutting up all the images she didn't approve. I liked her style. This girl was clearly in charge of her image.

WILLIAM

Around the time of 'Better the Devil You Know' there was a marked transition from the old bubblegum perm and dressing-up-box cuteness. Now, for the first time, Kylie was hot. Big bed-head hair, wigs inspired by Liz Taylor, Joan Collins and Jane Fonda, leopard fake furs, corsetry, feather boas, lashings of black eyeliner, panther tattoos... It was truly exciting to witness Kylie's transformation into a sex siren of almost drag queen sensibilities.

opposite

WILLIAM

As Kylie began to exert more control over her image, it seemed that overnight she grew up and discovered her sexuality. The girl next door was now wearing Galliano and writhing away with a bunch of muscled dancers!

KYLIE

John Galliano designed my entire wardrobe for the 'Let's Get To It' tour. At the time I loved wearing one of his floor-length skirts with strategically placed slashes.

above

KATERINA JEBB

Kylie is a born exhibitionist so it's obviously a lot of fun to photograph her. We met for the first time when she came to visit me at home in Paris in 1991. We opened a bottle of champagne and became firm friends.

KYLIE

Kat and I did lots of shoots at her apartment. This was taken by her front door in a favourite vintage dress and Robert Clergerie shoes. We had such freedom and always got into mischief.

KYLIE

We shot at a friend of Kat Jebb's in Romden, Kent.
We had outrageous fun but that is another story!
These photos are in my trusty Azzedine Alaïa once
again. I absolutely loved the flowery hair-do courtesy
of the legendary Sam McKnight and the make-up
by Sarah 'Flinty' Reygate.

SAM McKNIGHT

This was a lovely day in an old country house, with
Kylie playing around. As well as being incredibly
beautiful and talented, she is one of the most
gracious ladies I have had the pleasure of working
with, and she is extremely photogenic and always
up for trying a new look. She called me one Friday
night and said she wanted her hair short. Before I got
there she'd cut it off, so I gave her the elfin crop.

opposite & above

KYLIE

I loved my Hysteric Glamour mini dress shown opposite. I used to wear it out with little strappy hot pink heels. The shoot was elegant and cool in its simplicity. I remember Mary Greenwell going to town with the lip liner!

overleaf left

KYLIE

William styled this shoot but Kat Jebb and I were left to our own devices, as we shot in my London apartment. I did my hair and make-up, which was usually the case when Kat and I did a shoot. Very low-fi. I remember we thought it was so funny to put the posters of me above the bed, which were all shot by famous photographers with a big team, and there we were with one light that we lugged around and the bag of clothes Willie provided. In a way it had its own pseudo-punk spirit, which worked well with the Vivienne Westwood pieces.

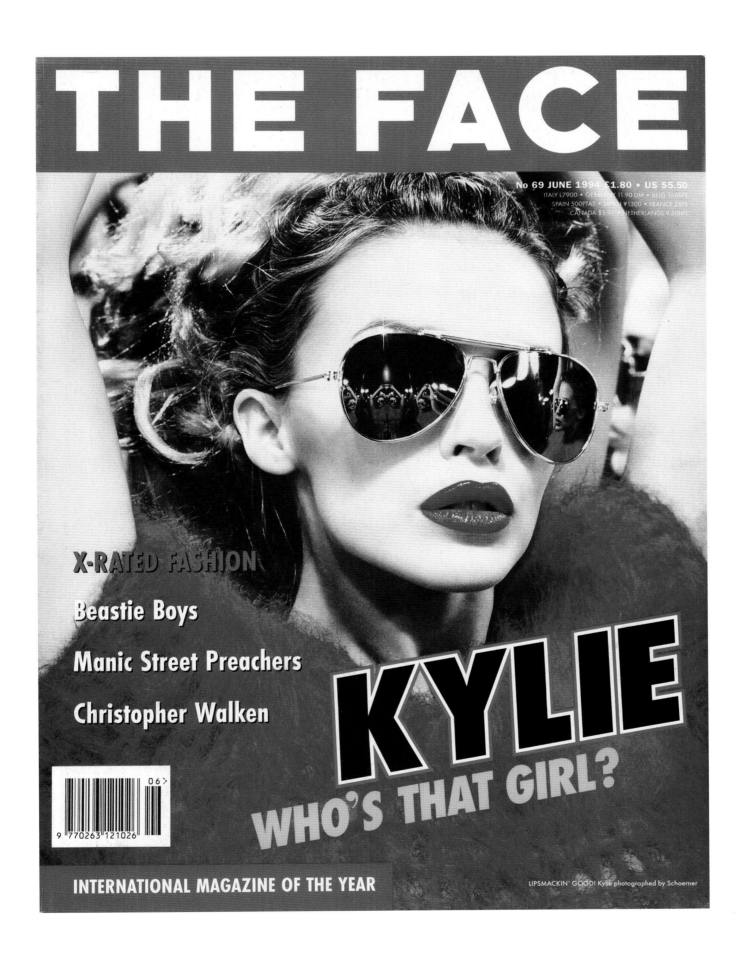

THE FACE

No 69 JUNE 1994 £1.80 • US $5.50
ITALY L7900 • GERMANY 11.90 DM • BELG 166FR
SPAIN 500PTAS • JAPAN ¥1300 • FRANCE 28FR
CANADA $5.95 • NETHERLANDS 9.50HFL

X-RATED FASHION

Beastie Boys

Manic Street Preachers

Christopher Walken

KYLIE
WHO'S THAT GIRL?

9 770263 121026 06>

INTERNATIONAL MAGAZINE OF THE YEAR

LIPSMACKIN' GOOD! Kylie photographed by Schoerner

KATIE GRAND

When I'd left *Dazed & Confused* and moved to
The Face, we put Kylie on the cover. It was the
best-selling issue during my tenure there.

KATIE GRAND

I very nearly didn't go to my first Kylie shoot. Rankin and I were dating and we had a huge fight the night before. I remember calling Jefferson Hack and he talked me round. I love working with Kylie, we've had some brilliant times together, and she really did end up changing my career. Thank you, Jefferson, for making me get on that plane to LA.

KYLIE

This shoot was exciting, as Rankin and Katie epitomized the fashion surge London was having. Their dynamism and 'cool' was exactly what I was attracted to at that time. It was the beginning of many things we did together down the line.

opposite & above

KATIE GRAND

Since Kylie was going through a bit of a transition from super pop to cool, Rankin and I thought it would be good to shoot her for a *Dazed & Confused* supplement, which we named 'the Kylie Bible'. I took a selection of my friends' clothes; I'd never really styled a big shoot and thought you just took a few things with you. I also put in a dark green Paul Smith women's suit at the last minute, which ended up being used for the album sleeve.

overleaf

KYLIE

Ellen von Unwerth and I have done so many photo shoots together, and her distinct style makes for a playful shoot. Also we always got so much done. I love how she encourages movement and freedom; letting your character shine through, or letting you have fun playing a character.

THE FUN ISSUE   NO.130

i-D

© i-DEAS, FASHION, CLUBS, MUSIC, PEOPLE

cover star: **kylie minogue** JULY 1994

£1.95 $4.95

07

9 770262 357013

FRANCS 35 LIRE 7,100 DM 13,00 PESETAS 595 D KR 53

**HARDWEAR:
SUMMER
DENIM SPECIAL**

Erasure
under analysis

Pedro Almodovar
master of sex'n'kitsch

Young Fuct
with LA's fashion outlaws

rural rebellion
the battle for Solsbury Hill

kylie
on top

Plus... L7 • freedom comes to South Africa • the best clubs, clothes & cybertech

above & opposite
KYLIE

I'm wearing Véronique Leroy. The shoot was so very difficult but we knew that once we got it right it would be amazing. All of the light effects were done in actuality, not post-production, so Stéphane was whizzing around me in black-out clothing as I tried my best to stay still for the long exposure. At the time I was wearing a lot of Junya Watanabe and Comme des Garçons. High heels took a back seat and I took on quite a boyish look, as Stéphane and I went on lots of adventures, like travelling on bicycles in China and driving across America.

STÉPHANE SEDNAOUI

Besides doing the 3D 'Impossible Princess' cover, which was technically complicated and physically very demanding for Kylie, all the other shoots we have done were always fun and easy. She has a wonderful positive energy.

overleaf
KYLIE

I did this shoot with Matt Jones in a car park in London. The dress was by Zan Burgess and I think the lingerie was Agent Provocateur. We were trying to get the shoot done without attracting too much attention, which isn't so easy when you're undressing, dressing and then undressing again!

centre left

PHILIP TREACY

It's exciting to design hats for royalty, and Kylie is the Queen of Pop!

opposite & above

WILLIAM

Owen Gaster was a really good friend and I loved his clothes. He was part of that amazing generation of London designers who changed the face of British fashion with their conceptual approach and masterful technical ability. Owen is the most incredible pattern cutter, and his suiting and tailoring was sexy and graphic, almost architectural; even reminiscent of the dynamics of sports car design. Kylie wore a green dress of his with devore beetles on the cover sleeve of 'Did It Again', and another with cut-out panels in this Jonathan West Polaroid. She also used to wear a totally see-through bright fluoro green lace shift dress that he made for her...with Nike trainers, of all things, and no bra, and somehow managed to look really cool. I had an aversion to girls in trainers at that time, thinking that all girls should be born with feet shaped like Barbie!

WILLIAM

Jonathan West was a photographer I was 'testing' with at the time, building up my portfolio. Kylie saw some of the pictures we'd done together and loved them, so we arranged a shoot. It took place not long after I'd finished university, in the flat I shared with my best friend in St Anne's Court, Soho. I painted each wall a different colour or put up wallpaper for each specific shot and got so carried away I accidentally kicked a can of red paint all over the student accommodation carpet. Kylie wore little or no make-up,

and the clothes came from friends of mine – Owen Gaster, Antonio Berardi and some bits of Véronique Leroy. It was such a great shoot: just three people with no preconceived ideas about what we were going to do, making it up as we went along, using everything that was in my bedroom. The student accommodation board freaked out when we moved out, as I never painted the room back. They freaked even more when they rolled back the rug and discovered a huge red paint stain in the middle of the carpet.

KYLIE

We wanted a completely different mood for this session. We succeeded, and I remember at the time not loving the look, as it was so strong. I don't think the grunge era really suited me, but now I think the pictures have a real freshness and I appreciate them in a new way.

KYLIE

I've now worked with Simon so many times over the years, but this was the first session. So much of what I was doing at this time had a tiny budget so I brought a lot of pieces, including the pink glitter sticky roll, from home. It was a great, simple shoot with a lot of heart.

SIMON EMMETT

Shot on a shoestring... This was inspired by Kylie's 'Cowboy Style' track, and also drew from Sam Haskins's book, *Cowboy Kate*. There are no fashion constraints with Kylie. Her natural poise and dynamism transcend all typical props and accessories. We've made great use here of our easy rapport.

LIZ COLLINS

Kylie dancing in front of the camera... It's incredible to be able to photograph someone who is so aware of their movement. We decided to use props – the hoola hoop ('spinning around'), bike, baseball glove, rollerblades – to give movement and fun. The shoot was to be up, smiling and joyful. Kylie was so open to play and collaborate. For me it was a real high. I fell in love. Who wouldn't?

KYLIE

With 'Spinning Around', it was time to be pop-tastic again. I had happily experimented with different styles, sounds and looks, as it gave me a new perspective, but I was ready to let the sunshine back in. Liz's aesthetic was very much about a natural beauty, and this session, although indoors, managed to capture the feel we were going for.

above

STELLA McCARTNEY FOR CHLOÉ

I was one of the designers to have a hot pant moment and that was with Kylie...now, not many can say that!

left

KATERINA JEBB

I found the gold hot pants at the North End Road market in London for 50 pence.

DAWN SHADFORTH

The record company brief on 'Spinning Around' was tanned, golden, happy, smiley Kylie. William came up with Studio 54 as a concept.

WILLIAM

Dawn's gorgeous video was an exercise in re-launching Kylie and showcasing her derrière, clad in gold, the colour of kings. We were inspired by campaigns for Stella McCartney and Chloé, which featured glorious sunsets and gorgeous, natural, tanned, blonde girls on the beach. Kylie here is the ultimate golden girl, with her Farrah Fawcett flick. She gleams on the screen, radiating youthful charisma, vitality and sex appeal. The infamous hot pants had their first outing at a 'Nerds, Tarts and Tourists' fancy dress party that Kylie attended. After that they resided undisturbed at the back of her sizeable knicker drawer for a couple of years until I pulled them out for Dawn to consider for the video. The rest is history.

VINCENT PETERS

The first time Kylie and I met was on this shoot for the 'Light Years' album in Ibiza. A memorable experience? The fact is that I came back to Ibiza and I never left again.

KYLIE

The shoot was incredible. It was my first album with Parlophone and we were very sure of the message we wanted to get across: sunshine, beach, fun, glamour. I've always loved Ibiza and it's true that the island has a magical quality. The lightness of the chiffon matched my mood and desire.

WILLIAM

These images have an almost mystical quality to them. It was no accident that Kylie, shot against blue skies and the blue horizon of the sea, was also wearing a blue chiffon swimsuit by Jeremy Scott. After Titian, the colour blue acquired an otherworldly quality often associated with the Virgin or Heaven itself, and Yves Klein used it centuries later to symbolize the great beyond. With 'Light Years' we wanted a cover that was a visual statement about Kylie reclaiming the throne of the Princess of Pop. Ibiza was perfect, as the Mediterranean home of dance music and euphoric hedonism. And so, surrounded by the infinity of blue sky and ocean, Kylie returned to her rightful place!

JULIEN MACDONALD

It feels like a lifetime that Kylie and I have been working together. She is my absolute favourite person to work with. She puts the bubbles in champagne! I have fantastic memories of working on tour costumes with her and William, particularly the 'On a Night Like This' tour, for which I designed and made the crystal-encrusted outfits below. For her performance at the Brits in 2003, Kylie wore a metal mesh-embellished mini dress that I designed. Justin Timberlake couldn't keep his hands to himself and pinched her famous bottom!

KYLIE

Julien has provided many a sparkle for me! One of his dresses had so many crystals and weighed so much it was near impossible to hold it with one hand. Of course once on the body it was a whole lot more manageable.

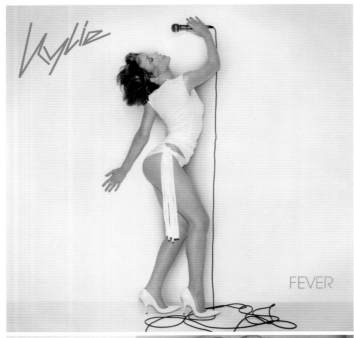

WILLIAM

Graphic designer Tony Hung and I came up with a creative brief that was about electro-minimalism. We shot Kylie bound by a microphone cord, literally tied to her craft. The shoes were made for her by her beloved Manolo Blahnik, and the all-white clothes were by Mrs Jones, whose designs came to symbolize this era of Kylie-ness.

KYLIE

The whole campaign was so strong, sure, ice cool. Willie's styling was incredible and Vincent Peters's photography made for a second amazing album cover with him.

MRS JONES

Kylie knows exactly how things are made, as her grandmother was a seamstress, so as I'm pinning one side she's pinning the other. You don't need much fabric for her, as she's so petite!

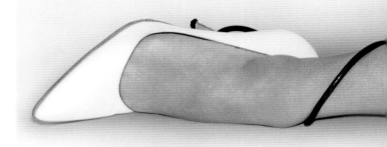

XEVI MUNTANE

I started my career thanks to Kylie. I must have been
22 years old when I first shot her. That says a lot about
her. Above is one of my favourite pictures of her. She
was moving quite a lot in some of the shots and I was
scared she would get tangled with all the neons that
were hanging on wires behind her and get electrocuted.
That would not have been good for my career! The
picture opposite was William's idea. At first I thought
it would come across as egocentric, but Kylie's charm
made it cheeky, funny and very sexy.

WILLIAM

I simply love Xevi. We met in a bar in Soho and became
partners in crime. He was just starting out, too. He came to stay
with me when he was in town from his native Barcelona and we
would shoot. He was and is a big fan of Kylie's, which is so nice
to work with, as he has such excitement about a project. He just
utters one word when he shoots – 'hot...hot...hot!' – which always
used to make us laugh. He has photographed Kylie many times
over the years and I love his images. They are always different
from others' images of her, because his adoration of her shines
through with such clarity.

DAWN SHADFORTH

I don't think there was a specific record company
brief for this video. It was a case of showing Kylie
and William the environments and discussing the
concept – that it was a kind of future utopia and
the characters were 'sensual drones'. I said I wanted
Kylie's performance to be strong, engaged with the
camera and predatory, so that must have fed in.
William came up with the idea of using Mrs Jones to
design outfits. Kylie knows what works for her body
and her personality, but she's also brave and playful
enough to try out new things just for the hell of it.
Her work has a sensibility that is entirely her.

MRS JONES

The moment this was first aired on TV I was with
my best mate. The camera started at Kylie's foot and
slowly slid up the body to the reveal. By the end we
were screaming like lunatics. Male or female, there
was not a person in the land at that point who didn't
get goose bumps or fancy Kylie Minogue.

KYLIE

The now iconic jumpsuit required more than one
'trick of the trade' to preserve my modesty! The outfit
is one of the many elements of that video that seemed
perfect. I can't imagine it never having existed.

DOLCE & GABBANA

Kylie is extremely professional, as well as a lovely and amazing person. It's great to work with her. Plus it's creatively stimulating. When we design something for her, we do our best to make sure it perfectly matches her artistic mood. It's important that she *feels* the outfit.

KYLIE

When I was younger, I always had to explain how to spell both 'Kylie' and 'Minogue'. Looking at the belt Dolce & Gabbana made for me, it's funny to think these names became so well known. Much of me is still the unknown girl with an unusual name.

opposite & right

KYLIE

This shoot with David LaChapelle in Los Angeles was *crazy*. I was in LaChapelle World! Extremely hard work, but worth it all. The set-ups and the fashion – Dior couture, Versace – were just sensational.

overleaf left

XEVI MUNTANÉ

The parrot we rented for the shoot was almost the size of Kylie herself. It would scream *soooo* loud once in a while, like it was being taken to the butcher's. Kylie in Versace remained strangely calm, with that heavy monster on her arm. She's a true professional. The bird also got obsessed with her lips and would try to poke her mouth every two minutes. It was hilarious and scary.

overleaf right

KYLIE

There was a lot of customization happening at the time, and this Noki T-shirt dress was a great piece.

MRS JONES

Looking back over the pictures of Kylie wearing
my designs, it just makes me feel so lucky and
thankful that she gave me a chance. That's the
great thing about the Kylie/William combo.
They keep it fresh and are always on the lookout
for something or someone new. They've given
a lot of young, undiscovered designers a break...
which is a wonderful, rare thing in my books.

KYLIE

Whenever there are 'rocks' on set, you can
be sure there are a couple of security guards
keeping a close eye on them.

WILLIAM

Kylie possesses that indefinable star quality
and charisma that is so often lacking in many
of her contemporaries.

above

WILLIAM

Johnny Rocket is a true craftsman. He created a series
of personalized, street-inspired jewelry for 'Fever',
consisting of items we'd used for the album shoot:
charm bracelets, necklaces and dog tags featuring
the silhouette from the album cover, tiny headphones,
Manolo's stilettoes, a microphone, 'K' tag earrings, this
knuckleduster of Tony Hung's electro Kylie logo, with
small diamonds, all crafted out of silver. Johnny also
created the 'KylieFever' tour 'Kyborg', its chrome layers
peeling off to reveal the Dolce & Gabbana silver-clad
space princess inside.

JOHNNY ROCKET

I remember how Kylie diffused the stress I was feeling
when she was to emerge out of the shell of the Kyborg,
as we could have electrocuted her! But maybe the
one image I will go to the grave with is of her in her
Manolos, covered in plaster of Paris when making the
Kyborg mould, and still having a laugh.

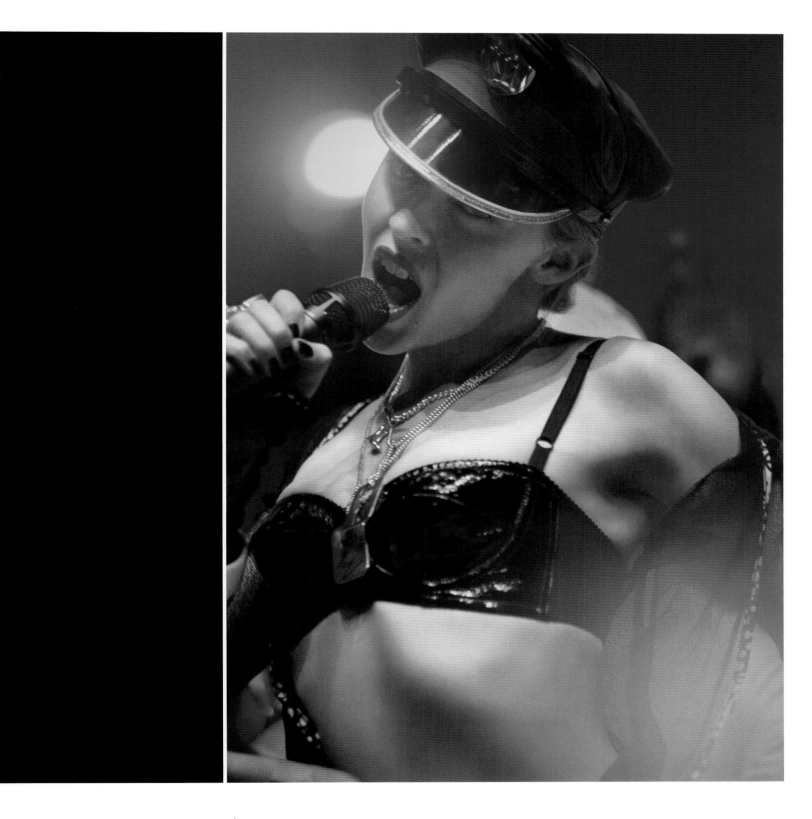

above

KYLIE

This photo was used for the cover of the amazing French magazine, *Numéro*. Apparently I was the first artist, i.e. non-model, to appear on the cover. The shot was taken on stage before soundcheck on the 'Fever' tour. Stéphane Sednaoui is such a visionary, and his photos are so distinctive and memorable.

STÉPHANE SEDNAOUI

I met Kylie for the first time for a music video project that we ended up not doing, but the time I *really* met Kylie was a few weeks later at *The Face* party in London on the 19th of July 1996. She was so unbelievably cute and petite that I suddenly ignored the crowd and, after asking her politely, lifted her in the air. Then I was in love.

KYLIE

I love these photos. I had just come off stage on the 'Fever' tour in Glasgow. Hot and exhausted. Not exactly when you feel like doing a photo shoot! Somehow I got all the clothes on and Stéphane took these in my dressing room. I think because of the circumstances they have a beautiful, lazy, elegant energy. The mask was one of my dancer's costumes, and I was wearing Dolce & Gabbana and Chanel.

KYLIE

The outfit for the 'Sex in Venice' section arrived as designed. Something didn't look right so I cut up the chiffon jacket to make lace cuffs and added layers to the pants. I remember my entire team frantically putting the final touches to everything, right up until going on stage on opening night. Yes, I stitched the changes to this outfit myself! Thankfully Stefano and Domenico understand that changes often need to be made once a costume is seen in its intended environment. Usually, it's adding sparkle or adjusting the means of getting in and out to shave valuable seconds off a 'quick change'. Working on a costume myself is a bonding process with what will effectively be my second skin on stage.

WILLIAM

Kylie loves Dolce & Gabbana, citing how amazing she feels when wearing their creations, with their in-built corsetry. The 'KylieFever' tour looks were inspired by the flesh satin corsetry of Venetian courtesans, the iconic look of the Droogs from *A Clockwork Orange*, the idea of a diamond-clad cyborg queen with her army of liquid metal drones and a burning voodoo-inspired goddess who dwelt inside the fiery depths of a volcano. The choreography by contemporary master Rafael Bonachela created a body language all of its own, which brought Dolce & Gabbana's creations to life.

DOLCE & GABBANA

DOLCE & GABBANA

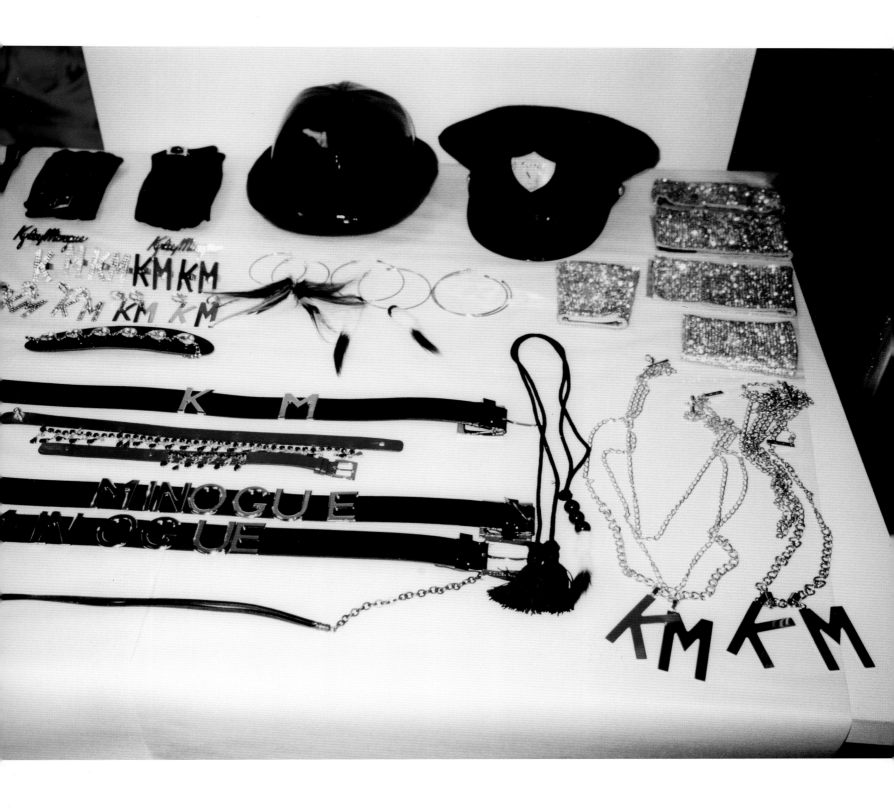

previous pages, opposite & above

KYLIE

I will always love and appreciate the costumes from my early days. My mum, grandmother and I would all be working on them. I remember fabric being laid over the kitchen table, the patterns being cut and the whirr of the sewing machine, beads being sewn and trimmings lovingly applied. Jump cut to working with Dolce & Gabbana on the 'Fever' tour and it was akin to the Industrial Revolution! There were endless pieces, doubles, triples, shoes, jewelry and more. It was like I had finally hit the big time. On top of that, Stefano and Domenico were such a delight to work with, and the results were outstanding.

WILLIAM

For the 'KylieFever' tour Dolce & Gabbana created a range of KM jewelry and belts with Kylie's name in gleaming gold letters. Every look had a KM signature piece of jewelry. They had such delight in playing with her name as part of the costumes, incorporating her into their world, and were so proud of the association, which remains delightful as there can often be a snobbery on the part of the fashion world towards pop. Dolce & Gabbana love dressing pop stars and through them their work reaches a much wider audience and can often truly inspire high street fashion in just as powerful a way as a catwalk show.

ALI MAHDAVI

I'm often asked who I've enjoyed shooting the most, and I always answer Kylie Minogue, even though I risk being strangled by my other muses! But it's true. I love her nose, and she has the most delicious and adorable body, like a delicate china doll, with gorgeous, tiny, irresistible hands and feet. We only had an hour and a half to shoot this series, including hair and make-up, but she was so strong, glamorous, intense and clever that we managed to do several different pictures. It was a nightmare to make a choice on the contact sheet: each take was perfect. I wanted to shoot in the spirit of Marlene Dietrich, to show a 'real woman' aspect of Kylie, not the usual girly baby-doll. While I was shooting, I suddenly realized that Kylie was much more Marilyn than Marlene. I screamed, 'Now I want you to be like Marilyn in the Avedon picture, where she looks depressed.' Not only did Kylie know what I was referring to, but she gave it to me in a second, and it blew my mind.

KYLIE

The allure of the corset will be eternal. Yes, they are uncomfortable, but for a short time – thanks to Mr Pearl – you have the most fantastical and entrancing figure. Shooting with Ali was an absolute delight. He used a little torch as the key light, which fascinated me. That prompted long chats, sharing our love of Hollywood golden era lighting.

KATIE GRAND

When I became editor of *Pop*, I wanted to work with Kylie again, to do something super-sexy and raunchy. We shot the pictures in Mert and Marcus's flat on Old Street in London, which didn't even have a real bathroom. I barely had any clothes with me, and thus Kylie didn't end up wearing much. I remember the biggest challenge was getting her to bleach her eyebrows. Eventually she gave in to much bullying from me, Charlotte Tilbury and Guido. The shoot ended at about three in the morning.

KYLIE

This shoot looks strong and serious, but working with Mert and Marcus is always fun. They have a great energy, and such vision and style. Katie and I had by now worked together quite a lot, and, once again, she produced something fresh and exciting.

opposite
KYLIE

This Mert and Marcus photo was an homage to my
mum, Carol. I have a beautiful photo of her as a
teenager, by a similar tree, wearing her dancing outfit.
I've always loved it and been slightly obsessed with
recreating it. I don't think I can ever be as beautiful
as she is in that photo but this one comes close and
makes me happy, feeling that link to my mum.

above
KYLIE

I met Nicolas Ghesquière at Balenciaga to fit the
dress for the 'Slow' video, which was an absolute
masterpiece. After that I wore a lot of the daywear,
like the jacket above. I still have this and wear it
often. The boots were one of my vintage finds.

WILLIAM

Mert and Marcus are masters of modern fashion
photography. There are few fashion photographers
who can interpret a reference from the past and make
it relevant like they can. Their sense of exaggerated
but refined glamour and sexuality is unsurpassed,
and they can turn their talents to creating and
harnessing any look from any period of fashion
history. Perhaps more than any other photographers
we have collaborated with, they approach their work
with an incredible understanding of the minutiae and
precision of styling, hair and make-up.

KYLIE

I love this photo in the cornfields. This entire session with Mert and Marcus was so much fun. We raced around for two days in the South of France and the shoot was epic. Here, I was dancing around in the sunset wearing Chanel lace gloves (which I also wore for the 'Money Can't Buy' concert for the 'Body Language' album) and a spectacular Judy Blame bra. Judy is an institution of London fashion and has made so many beautiful pieces for me. When we met, it was in the wake of Ray Petri and the Buffalo era. Judy was and remains the real deal, hand-crafting art pieces imbued with the punk aesthetic that originally inspired him.

JUDY BLAME

The first time I met Kylie was after her 'Hit Factory' period. She wanted to feel more groovy and I was brought in to polish up her credibility a bit. I loved accessorizing her and the dancers for a one-off gig at G-A-Y. We got the cover of *QX* and tons of press, so I was thrilled. It's always a pleasure working for Kylie and her team. Professional good fun!

WILLIAM

Judy Blame – jewelry designer, fashion stylist and general 'leg-end', as he describes himself – has been a long-time hero of mine. I grew up with his styling collaborations with Boy George and Neneh Cherry in the late 1980s/early '90s, when I first became aware of 'stylists' working behind the scenes. I met him through mutual friend Philip Treacy some time after he had directed Kylie's first *i-D* shoot. He is the consummate craftsman, slaving away for hours with a needle and thread and anything from champagne corks and dominos to designer carrier-bag ribbons, shoelaces and shards of smashed LPs. His work has its own graphic iconography. Each piece has the power to define and create a look and a photograph, the jewelry or accessories often being art pieces themselves. Over the years he has created so much for Kylie: berets embroidered with his signature black-and-white buttons; badges for 'Body Language Live'; the chain and LP shard corset worn for the 'Body Language' cover shoot; pocket accessories worn for 'Red Blooded Woman' and 'Timebomb'; the Pearly Queen jacket and hat he created for Kylie's performance at the Queen's Jubilee concert in London in 2012... Judy is a true visionary, and a wit to boot.

opposite
KYLIE

I wished I had been a Chloé girl at this time. I wore
enough of it that I practically was, in my own way.
I had been to the studio in Paris some time before
this and met Stella McCartney. For me, Chloé was
absolutely wearable, feminine 'cool'. All you had
to do was put it on.

below & overleaf left
KYLIE

Much of this shoot was an homage to Brigitte Bardot.
I was really into finding a sexy look while being
quite covered up, hence ever-present black opaque
tights. The top on the next page is classic Jean Paul
Gaultier and the amazing chain suspenders were by
Johnny Rocket.

WILLIAM

Mert and Marcus's women have a strength and power
to them that I love. In my opinion, these Bardot-inspired
images are some of the best photographs of Kylie ever.
She adopted a heavily referenced guise and made it her
own. Bardot is one of the many twentieth-century film
icons that Kylie has been inspired by over the years.
At this point in her life, Kylie was almost quintessentially
Parisian and loved all things French...hence the striped
Gaultier sweater and the shoot's glamorous, sunny
location in the South of France, which no doubt brought
the Bardot-inspired character to life.

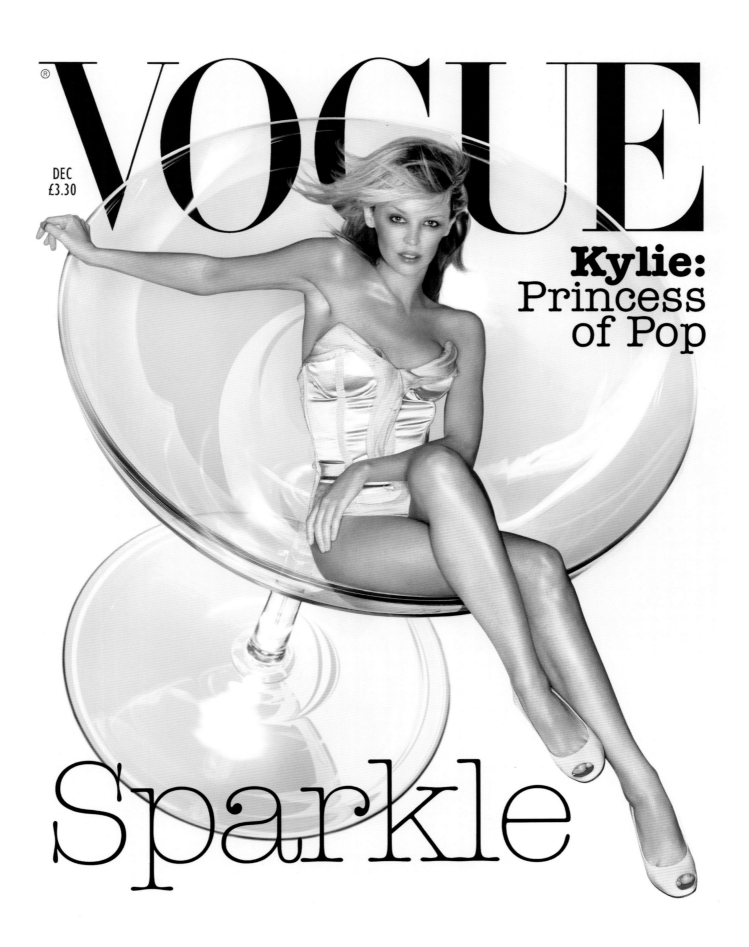

VOGUE

DEC
£3.30

Kylie:
Princess
of Pop

Sparkle

KYLIE

This *Vogue* cover photographed by Nick Knight is one of my favourite covers. I love the colour palette, the gorgeous Stella McCartney body, the Louboutin heels, perched in a champagne glass. Perfect!

above
KYLIE

I'm wearing Helmut Lang, Chanel and Judy Blame. I met Helmut Lang at his store in New York. As a long-time fan this was a real treat. He created looks for the 'Money Can't Buy' concert and an amazing couture horsehair and chiffon dress in red for the 'Chocolate' video.

opposite
LAUDOMIA PUCCI

I remember a special 'private' fashion moment in Portofino when I first met Kylie. She was wearing an enormous Pucci printed hat and sitting on a yacht that Pucci had customized. A special lady. A unique pop star. The Mediterranean sea and a designer sailboat. The beginning of a great friendship!

KYLIE

Pucci prints make me feel joyful. Among many Pucci moments with the legendary Pucci house were the giant 'wings' they created for the 'Showgirl' tour. I felt like I literally was floating, with reams of delicious Pucci chiffon around me.

previous pages

previous pages

KYLIE

This shoot was with Kat Jebb in the Bois de Boulogne outside Paris. All the clothes are vintage. Kat and I used to spend hours at local markets, searching for great finds. She would always, always find the best pieces for a few euros!

above

RICHARD NICOLL

This dress is from the first capsule collection I did when I left my MA. I accosted William in Soho and introduced myself, and from then on he and Kylie have been constant supporters. I love dressing Kylie because she's fearlessly experimental. She's cheeky (in more ways than one)!

opposite

KYLIE

I adore these pieces by Nicolas Ghesquière at Balenciaga. Both were so intricate, yet light to wear. Sexy and strong.

WILLIAM

Nicolas's designs at the time had an almost science-fiction, robotic futurism to them and really pushed at boundaries of form. They were often made in oceanic tones out of sportswear fabrics – nylons, neoprene. At the same time they always retained the original chic of the Balenciaga house, with gorgeous lines and seams that elongated the body and created a powerful silhouette. We worked with Balenciaga a lot at the time of 'Body Language'.

opposite
KYLIE
This was taken at the end of the day in the sunlight streaming through a London photo-studio window. It was a cover shoot for *i-D* magazine and of course you always have to come up with a way to wink or cover one eye. This time we shadowed!

above
WILLIAM
These images come from two shoots, about two weeks apart. What makes me laugh is they show how schizophrenic we are, as there are three or four *totally* different looks here. They show how different Kylie can look, not just over the course of 25 years, but over two weeks or even one afternoon. Hairdresser Johnnie Sapong went to town with the wigs, and the photographer, Tesh, just got quieter, probably thinking, 'Who are these nut jobs?' The shots show what an actress Kylie is in front of the camera with her facial expressions and body language. Her features can carry off virtually any look and bring any character to life.

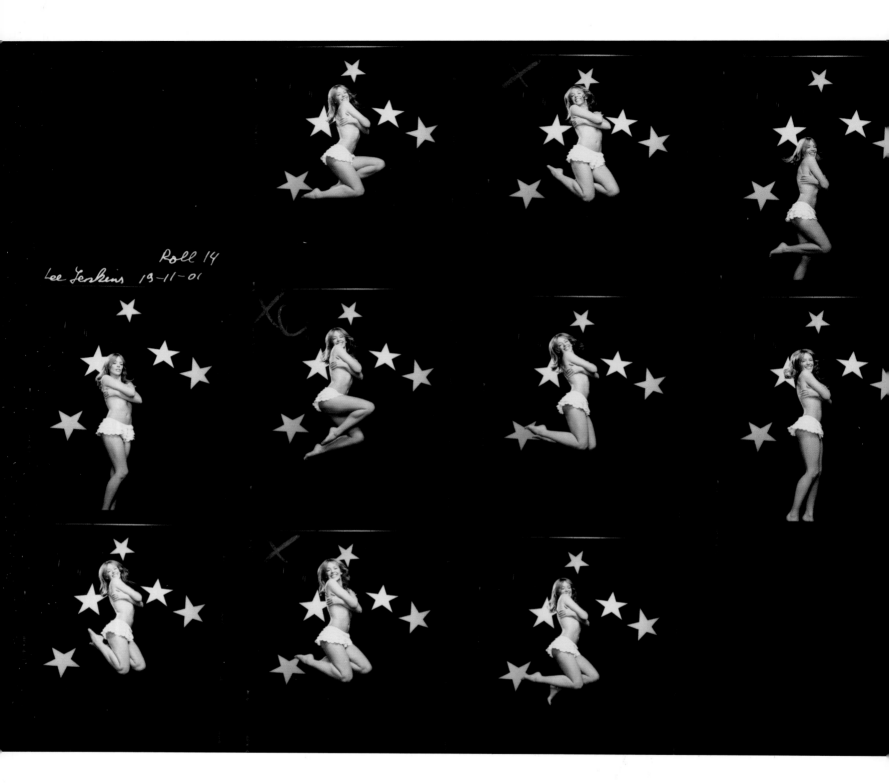

Roll 14

Lee Jenkins 19-11-01

KYLIE

This was such a fun shoot. I posed with lots of different flat props, including straddling a rocket, hah! For the shot with the stars I was bouncing up and down in gorgeous Chloé shorts on a trampette. There was also the cute white rabbit, whose hidden claws were quite a challenge to deal with. I was in love with all of my Johnny Rocket jewelry. He crafted so many gorgeous, cool pieces for me, including the 'Fever' logo bracelet. Oh, and the teddy polar bear went missing, i.e. it came home with me!

JOHNNY ROCKET

Kylie and William have created a formidable team and
a gigantic cultural icon. Kylie is also completely erudite
on fashion, all music, theatre, film... I've learned how much
effort, detail and commitment she puts into everything.
She and William were the first to send flowers to my wife
after the birth of our Ruby – in the midst of all the chaos.

KYLIE

Working with divine Simon Emmett again... We did this
shoot in an old house in Southeast London. We used
lots of different fashion, including Dolce & Gabbana,
La Perla, Antonio Berardi, Manolo Blahnik and finally
Willie's ex-boyfriend's grey T-shirt.

PIERRE BAILLY

I photographed Kylie for this couture story, shot in Coco Chanel's apartment on rue Cambon in Paris. We had no more than a couple of hours. I used that as an excuse to ask the team to wait outside so I could be alone with Kylie. From the moment she walked in, it felt as if she owned the place, or maybe it was the other way around – as if she was taken over by it. It was so inspiring to see her genuine excitement about each piece of couture and the history of the apartment, the woman and the fashion house.

KYLIE

This felt like a 'Once in a Lifetime' day. Exploring Coco Chanel's apartment and wearing exquisite Chanel couture... As a reaction to the grandeur, Katie Grand wanted the shoot to be lo-fi, so I did my hair and make-up, and I believe it was all shot in natural daylight. It was a very gentle shoot and Pierre was just lovely.

KYLIE

Xevi and I went pin-up-tastic for this shoot.
I adored the banana body so I purchased the
dress version (which I still have). Although
the pose looks light as air, on the inside I was
grimacing, as I must have done the equivalent
of a week's worth of sit-ups...

XEVI MUNTANÉ

I can certify that no one strikes a better pin-up
pose than Kylie. She totally knew how to work
that Chloé banana outfit. She knows how to
work her bananas!

KYLIE

I was wearing my 'Love Kylie' lingerie range, rolling
around on a sheepskin rug. This was a story for
Australian *Vogue* and, as always, Simon Emmett made
it very easy for me. The range was a great success
and a big learning curve for me about retail fashion.
Girls still tell me how much they adored 'Love Kylie'.

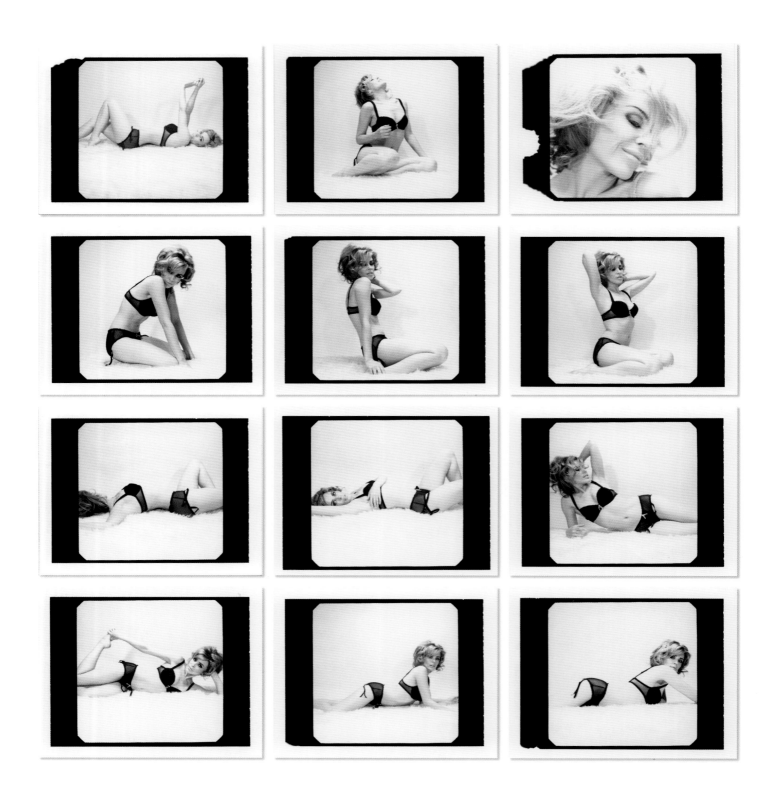

KYLIE

When I first spent time in Paris, I became an Azzedine
Alaïa addict. Buying his clothing and shoes was always
a major dent in the purse, but there was absolutely
nothing sexier at that time. I wore Azzedine faithfully
both on and off duty. To fit this dress I went to see him
at his studio. It's always such an honour to spend time
with him. He is inspiring and lovely, and his creations
are truly beautiful. White always works well on me
and this Grecian-inspired mini dress helped to lift
my spirits, as I remember I wasn't feeling so well this
particular day.

opposite & above

KYLIE

I had purchased a Chanel jacket in my early 20s.
It felt like the most glamorous rite of passage.
When I eventually met Karl Lagerfeld and visited
his studio, it was like a girl's dream come true. This
shoot was the first time he photographed me. I was
welcomed into his home in Paris, where we did the
shoot. I was so worried about scratching the piano
by lying on it, but Karl didn't seem to mind at all.
He is so full of life it's very inspiring. Even though
he had numerous assistants, he himself lifted me up
onto the mantelpiece for one of the shots! He gave
me some beautiful large prints from this shoot.

KARL LAGERFELD

What I like about photographs is that they capture a
moment that's gone forever, impossible to reproduce.

overleaf

KYLIE

William was photographing the 'Showgirl' brochure,
so there were plenty of feathers to deal with. For
some yin to the yang, we wanted a few shots with
more of a street style and naturalness, not to
mention some Balenciaga. For me it was a moment
of liberation from all the showgirl costumes I'd been
wearing that day.

JOHN GALLIANO

Kylie is a true Showgirl and Pop Pin-Up. I loved being part of such a triumphant and glamorous tour! It was Mae West, Moulin Rouge and more...

WILLIAM

This blue showgirl costume was based on an outfit that I fell in love with from John Galliano's 'Circus' collection. Fashion in our shows has always been interpreted through the angle of costume. The idea is to present Kylie in differing roles or guises throughout the various themes and acts of the live presentation. Everything about a Kylie show is exaggerated and fantastical, and her costumes have provided us with some of our finest and fondest fashion moments.

KYLIE

John Galliano created one of my most iconic looks. This was such an incredible costume, and every night on stage I knew the audience just loved it. Complete with my little strappy custom-made Manolo Blahniks, towering headgear by Stephen Jones and corset by Mr Pearl, it thrilled not only the crowd but me, night after night. For the quick change, the lacing at the back had to be cut. I suffered plenty of cuts on my arms until I figured out how to move and do the choreography while avoiding the sharp diamante stars. It was hard to move and hard to breathe, but it was such an amazing and resplendent moment I would brave it all again!

WILLIAM

John Galliano is the ultimate theatrical designer. His creations have a drama and an immaculate beauty all of their own. When his fashion genius was added to Kylie's on-stage persona, the results were stunning: a shimmering, shimmying showgirl queen, exuding glamour from every feather, every precisely placed crystal glittering under the lights. And uniquely Kylie. I can't imagine anyone else owning the showgirl guise as well as she does.

STEPHEN JONES

I remember fitting Kylie's hat and tail for this fabulous outfit. Strutting around her kitchen when she was trying it on for the first time...it looked more amazing than any of us could ever have imagined.

KYLIE

The artistry and craftsmanship that go into each and every couture creation truly amazes me – the hours, the love, the attention to detail. Once the designer's and artisans' work is done, my job is to bring that costume to life. Stephen's showgirl crown and bustle were just splendid. He had to be mindful of the need for me to be able to walk and balance. I did my best to make the waist on the corset as tiny as possible to please the ever-gentle Mr Pearl. Of course I had to make a small compromise in order to be able to sing.

for Kylie
with
love

previous pages

KYLIE

I visited Karl Lagerfeld at the Chanel studio in Paris and talked him through the idea of singing on a glittering half-moon in the 'Showgirl' tour. He sketched the design right there in front of me and it was magical. In the show I wore it on the crescent moon, singing 'Somewhere Over the Rainbow', and another great moment was on a revolving tiered circular stage for 'I Believe in You'. The structured front twinkled, and each tiny peach feather on the dress and train was fastened with a single crystal. I felt like a princess.

above & opposite

KYLIE

When Karl photographed me in Paris for *Elle* magazine, I asked him and his assistant what kind of look they wanted, and the reply was, 'You'. It was really refreshing to have that freedom and simplicity. I had fun wearing Armani Privé and a Lanvin dress, albeit back to front!

overleaf

KYLIE

When I stepped back in front of the camera after heavy medical treatment, I'm not sure if I was ready but I was eager. I wanted to put more distance between me and the past. Interestingly, a lot of the looks at that time were very heavy. This may have been a reaction to how I had felt during treatment – fragile, scared, and weak and blank. The make-up and costume acted a little like armour for me, offering protection and something sure, something certain. By now I knew that the 'Showgirl' tour was to be revived as 'Showgirl Homecoming'. I could start to feel the performer in me wanting to come out again.

WILLIAM

We did the shoot at The Lido cabaret theatre in Paris. We had previously used costumes from their archive, so it was a safe place for this major return in front of the camera lens. Kylie's energy was incredible, showing no obvious outward signs of her ordeal beyond her short cropped hair.

opposite & below

KYLIE

overleaf left

GARETH PUGH

overleaf right

KYLIE

This was a strong 'Joan of Arc' look and it was kind of how I was feeling at the time. I had been fighting and digging deep for strength. I also had to be a good leader, to show my family, my friends, my team that we would all get through this. Dolce's collection suited this spirit perfectly.

More or less as soon as my very first show at London Fashion Week was over I had to begin making costumes for the 'Showgirl' tour. It was the first time I'd ever worked on something on that scale, and it was amazing to see all that hard work come to life.

Gareth's designs are technical brilliance disguised as fantasy. I love taking on a different character with each look. The dark harlequin with Manolo Blahniks; the gold leather wig created by Eugene Souleiman...

left & above

WILLIAM

These shots were for the 'Homecoming' tour brochure and featured a darker, moodier Kylie than on the previous 'Showgirl' tour, though that infectious smile could still appear. In addition to McQueen, the Paris houses Chanel and Balenciaga seemed obvious choices for Kylie, who has always adored the city and who chose it as the place in which to undergo much of her post-cancer treatment. Her then-boyfriend Olivier Martinez and long-time friend Katerina Jebb had taken pictures of her since her illness, and it was to her friends that she turned more than ever in this difficult period. What strikes me about most of the images I took of her during this time is a strength and hardness that is a marked difference from the more playful, flirtatious sex kitten captured by others. Kylie is a survivor and possesses an almost inhuman strength contained within that diminutive frame.

KYLIE

I first met Alexander McQueen through Katie Grand. They were both over at my apartment to talk about a design. He was a brilliant designer and his fashion shows were always able to transport you to another place. The dresses here felt gladiatorial, which helped me to feel strong. As we were at The Lido, we styled them with a lot of the showgirls' crowns and accessories.

previous pages

KYLIE

When William put this look together, I thought he
had lost his mind! But the combination of Balenciaga,
leopard tights and Givenchy shoes looked great.
I was probably thankful for a lie-down, as we shot
intensively for three days at The Lido.

opposite & above

WILLIAM

Stage costumes emphasize and embellish Kylie's
shape and movement. She once said how, when
wearing each different outfit, she adopts a different
walk and body language to bring the costumes to
life. Nowhere was this more obvious than when she
wore the two glorious 'showgirl' looks created for her
by John Galliano. She strutted around that stage like
a rare bird of paradise, trailing sumptuous feathers
behind her stilettoed feet. The intricate feather crowns
and tiny corseted waists gave her a posture and
demeanour that appeared truly regal, as she had to
walk dead straight to keep the oversized plumes from
tumbling to the stage.

opposite, above & overleaf

WILLIAM

On stage, Kylie interprets clothes as part of
a character and uses them to add another layer
of spectacle. Dolce & Gabbana came up with the
leopard catwoman look when we were sat around
a table at their headquarters in Milan.

DOLCE & GABBANA

From the street look to total leopard print, Kylie has
always interpreted looks with a unique personal touch.

KYLIE

The showgirl was back. I loved the feather mohawk
skull cap and patent leather combination. It had
attitude. Then – a fan favourite, as well as one of
mine – the leopard catsuit, complete with little ears
and boxing gloves. It was so cute and foxy at the
same time. I prowled around the stage, which was
amped up further when Bono from U2 joined me one
night in Sydney to sing 'Kids', my duet recorded with
Robbie Williams.

WILLIAM

Gareth Pugh was introduced to me by Judy Blame just
after he'd finished college. The costumes he created
for Kylie are so three-dimensional, playing with form
and shape. The gold one is like an explosion of shards
of gold. The other, made from tiny cut-out squares
of white patent leather and bonded light-reflective
silver fabric, is like a human mirror ball, which Kabuki
enhanced with glitterball face make-up. Another
version of this dress, with metallic pink squares and
cowl, was used for the 'In My Arms' video. The work
that goes into Gareth's creations is astounding: an eye
for detail and originality matched by his charm and
sense of fun.

GARETH PUGH

My favourite Kylie moment? I think it has to be when
she came to DJ at my after-party in London. She wore
a dress that we had sent her straight off the runway –
a tight, black, leather, fringed number. She ended up
singing while catwalking up and down on top of the
bar, like a ghetto version of 'Spinning Around'!

KYLIE

We made golden leather fringe boots to match the
gold mini dress. Along with the Andy Warhol tribute
wig, it was a fun look to wear. The checkerboard
dresses Gareth made me were so striking, too.
With Kabuki's amazing full-face make-up, I was
coming close to being a human disco ball!

WILLIAM

John Galliano designed this outfit for an Eastern-inspired
section of the 'Homecoming' tour, choreographed by
contemporary master Akram Khan. Stephen Jones made
the golden-beaded orchid headpiece. This section marked
the first time that Kylie went back to work after her illness.
The contrast between this and the salmon pink showgirl
outfits couldn't be greater or more different in tone or design,
but we wanted the show to describe a journey and show that
the girl under the magnificent finery was really this very
humble, barefoot human being. The dress was exquisite,
with layers and layers of flesh chiffon beaded around the
edges, making Kylie appear almost nude from a distance
and making her seem even more ethereal and wraith-like
when she danced barefoot across the stage.

opposite

KABUKI

opposite

KABUKI

At our first informal one-on-one meeting, Kylie quickly made some astute selections of the ideas that I'd presented in the form of sketches. Some of the looks required pre-made accessories, so I taped bits of tracing paper to the outline of her eyebrows and eyes and traced over them with a pencil. The blue look is from the first shoot that we did. The mermaid eye pieces were made to measure by me the day before out of painted cardboard, fine tulle and Swarovski crystals. The crystal and beaded 'water' streaming from her silver-painted fingers was also hand-made (I got some help from last-minute recruits). The result was very Erté – not very practical, but pure fantasy.

above

KABUKI

For the zig-zag eye, there was no planning on my part at all. We had half an hour before we had to be done and William wanted another look. This meant I had to change the last make-up into something else...in about 15 minutes. Maybe it was the giant prop flower on the set that made me think along the lines of a bee and its sting. I only had time to do one eye, but I think it works better that way.

KYLIE

Kabuki is nothing short of a genius. The one thing you need is patience! He transforms the self you have always known right before your eyes. Through make-up he creates magic, fantasy, art.

previous page left

KABUKI

Kylie is the ultimate dress-up doll. It's so much fun to
see how she brings transformations to life. This look
was also from our first shoot. I originally made the
mask for a fashion show in New York. The patterned
net was created by carefully dabbing black nail polish
in the spaces between the netting and letting it dry
overnight. I didn't know at the time that it was destined
for the 'X' CD cover. The beauty mark is actually a
tiny star from the manicurist's kit that I painted black
(Kylie's idea).

previous page right

KABUKI

I was pleasantly surprised that Kylie picked this look
from my sketch ideas because it's definitely 'out there'.
Special-effects bald caps are always tricky to do,
involving lots of time for applying and removing, so
we did this look at the end of the day. Fortunately Kylie
is a pro, so I was able to do a good job on the cap and
not get any rips in it. The inspiration was part Leigh
Bowery, part Flintstones.

KYLIE

Considering my hair had not long ago grown back,
it felt a little weird – confronting – to be in a skull cap.
But I took it as a way of 'owning' the look, of making it
fun and strong, and of appreciating the beauty in it.

opposite & above

DANILO

Working on hair with Kylie is always inspiring and energizing, as she is a consummate professional. Her stellar show-business flair and gilded voice create pop icon perfection! She's never limited by boundaries and is always expanding and refreshing her vision and accomplishments. Last but not least she's a knockout. Gorgeous. Adorable. In a word, love!

KYLIE

Danilo and Kabuki make a magical team. We all love being together and having the opportunity to create fantastical looks. The first geisha look Danilo created for me was for the video for my duet with Japanese artist Towa Tei, 'G.B.I.', shot in New York and directed by Stéphane Sednaoui. We raced all over town, with me in full geisha outfit, fitted by a traditional Japanese dresser. The wig, resplendent with all its accoutrements, weighed a ton, so I had to prop my forehead on my wrist and try to convince myself I was resting.

below
KYLIE

I remember thinking how high-cut the graphic
Dsquared2 one-piece was. I was thankful for the
added protection of their great armour accessories!

opposite
WILLIAM

I was inspired by something that the media called
'the Kylie effect' after her diagnosis, which witnessed
unprecedented numbers of women going for breast
cancer check-ups. The support and overwhelming
public affection for her was incredible. I wanted to
do an image that showed her as the survivor and
inspiration she had become – thus the almost brazen
confidence and the Dolce & Gabbana hand-made
sequin top, with the lines of the sequins creating the
breasts. One of the most upsetting things I witnessed
in Kylie was her lack of body confidence after being
physically battered by therapies. I wanted to show that
sex appeal is not just skin deep; that it comes from
within. Kylie's strength and courageousness made her
more sexy to me, if anything. Kylie is a true beauty of
the age, blessed with both an outer and inner beauty.

below & opposite

VINCENT PETERS

Kylie is more elegant than most cover models, knows her body and is very patient. There's that Louis Malle film with Bardot where they say, 'Something happens between her and the camera that makes people want to look at her.' I think with Kylie it's the same. Sometimes, something happens.

KYLIE

I love wearing white or cream, and this story was so soft and lovely. It's such a pleasure to work with Vincent. Here he shot on film, which added to the feel of old-school glamour.

overleaf

KYLIE

Yves Saint Laurent can provide instant chic. As with any house, you have to choose the right pieces, but I have a staple of beautiful, timeless YSL in my wardrobe and they are just wonderful. The star collection here was more of a statement piece: different coloured Perspex stars and shapes linked together à la Paco Rabanne.

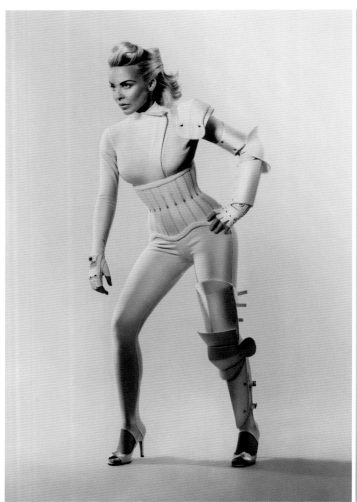 

above

STEVIE STEWART

I first started working with Kylie when William approached me to make a dress for her. It was very theatrical and made up with many different fabrics – brocade, gold net, red tulle, lots of bows: everything but the kitchen sink! These days everything I make for Kylie has a much more refined feel and a couture edge, even if it's a simple catsuit like this one, which we call the 'Fencing Suit'. It's one of many I've designed and made for Kylie over the years. I'm often referred to as the Queen of Lycra! I love getting outfits right for Kylie and it's a pleasure to see her wear them. I look forward to the fitting with her and we often have a giggle. She's so professional and knows a lot about fit, fabric and of course style. She can turn something as simple as this catsuit into an iconic fashion statement.

KYLIE

Stevie has designed and made countless outfits and props for me, including the giant shell for my stage entrance on the 'Aphrodite Les Folies' tour. Her wealth of experience and talent is incredible. She even has a tailor's dummy made to my proportions at her studio. Having worked extensively for dance companies, she fully appreciates what a performance outfit often requires.

opposite

MEADHAM KIRCHHOFF

I think, when I was making this dress, I was thinking that I wanted Kylie to look like a present!

opposite & above

MEADHAM KIRCHHOFF

These outfits were for 'The Kylie Show'. We made
the pointy-shouldered glittery jacket into an all-in-
one, and we made the Kylie-ized version of a gold
and black asymmetric dress from our Summer 2008
collection by turning it into an all-in-one showgirl
situation with a long train at the back.

KYLIE

Ed Meadham has made me many a beautiful,
striking outfit, and it's been joyful to watch his
work and talent shine with Meadham Kirchhoff.

overleaf

WILLIAM

Working with Jean Paul Gaultier was simply a dream
come true. Kylie was naturally in a darker place than
usual, and Jean Paul's avant-garde designs were
perfect for this 'darker' Kylie. The masked image
is my favourite photograph I have taken of her.
The outfit was inspired by elaborate Black Madonna
religious icons. There's something very powerful
about the eyes and their razor-sharp lashes staring
out at you, and the fact that the mouth is covered.
The skeleton dress Jean Paul made out of chiffon
was exquisite.

above, opposite & overleaf

WILLIAM

I am so proud of the 'X' tour images: Kylie literally riding death itself, as she entered the arena on a giant silver skull, or Kylie poised like a geisha… When she and Stéphane Sednaoui were going out together, they reminded me of characters from a Japanese anime or manga cartoon. Jean Paul Gaultier's creation for the tour was more of an anime multicultural geisha, with elements borrowed from Tibet, Mongolia and the whorehouse. There were stockings of thick French lace over a Japanese tattoo-print body suit. The obi from the waist was dropped a few centimetres and became a skirt that barely covered anything. The back of the outfit was incredible, with a corset spine down the back and straps that dissected Kylie's body. It's a costume for stage that is part of a much bigger theatrical context and picture, and, teetering on Giuseppe Zanotti shoes that were *so* high, Kylie looked just wonderful.

JEAN PAUL GAULTIER

When I had the opportunity to work with Kylie and William on their costumes for the world tour in 2007, I was very excited and enjoyed it so much. Kylie knew what she wanted and what she didn't. She was extremely precise and professional. She was always kind, happy and positive, with never a bad thought on her mind. Haute couture fittings are long and she would stand still for hours, very beautiful and always smiling, very much concentrating on 'the action'...

KYLIE

My friendship with Jean Paul has gone back a long way. I used to wear his hot-pant jumpsuits, Breton tops and corset tops back at the start of the '90s. Working with him on all my costumes for the tour was such a beautiful experience. Being in his presence is always inspiring and fun...not to mention the tempting sweets he normally brings to the fittings.

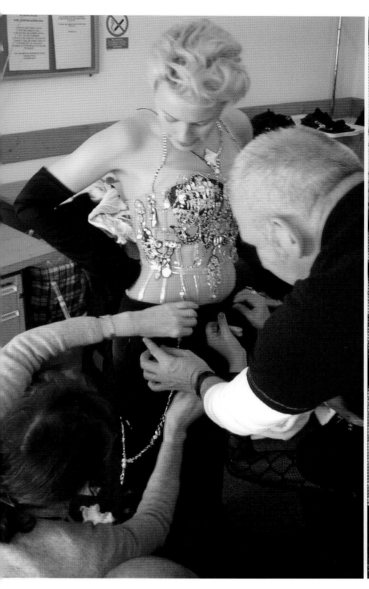

opposite

NATASHA LAWES

William Baker came across my 'Swarovski Crystal & Pearl Phantom' mask. What I think fulfilled the styling brief well was its luxurious nature. Clusters of different-sized jewels gave it an organic feel, and Swarovski crystal sparkles on stage like no other! The one-sided form added to the glamorous cyber/futuristic feel that William was creating for the shows, and the mask didn't cover too much of Kylie's face. I did have to make a second 'lighter' version for the stage performances, as the first version was quite heavy to wear for long periods. To see Kylie breathe life into one of my pieces was a real honour.

below

KYLIE

The detail in all Jean Paul Gaultier's couture pieces is mindblowing, and they are always an honour to wear. Jean Paul is a consummate artist. His enthusiasm about life in general is infectious, and as a bonus he is a super-fan of pop music!

Jean Paul Gaultier for Kylie.

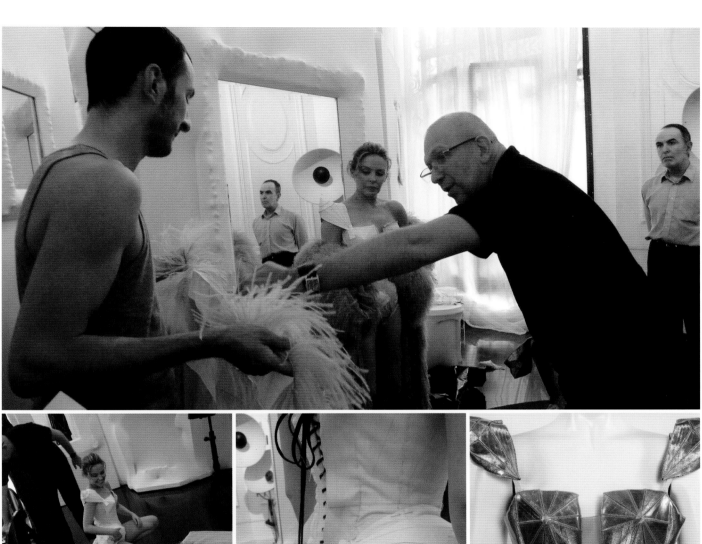

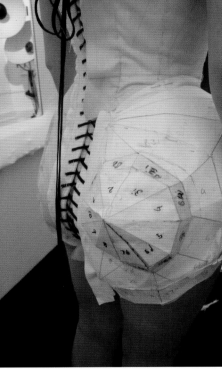

previous pages, opposite & above

KYLIE

To be with Jean Paul while he works is just amazing.
I watch his every move. I follow his eyes as they assess
what is and isn't working about the costume. He cuts,
drapes, adds, rips and pins until he is happy and he
knows that I am happy.

WILLIAM

The corset was like a geometric jigsaw puzzle. Its
padded hip panels and pointed bullet breasts distorted
the body shape. It was made from an iridescent fabric
covered in transparent plexi or plastic, and so rigid
it could stand upright. Kylie was the ultimate space
warrior queen, constellations revolving around her
head – a wire headpiece with tiny planets designed
by Stephen Jones. It was simply out of this world.

STEPHEN JONES

The first time I met Kylie I was completely star struck and, to tell you the truth, I still am! But my favourite Kylie fashion moment was putting a giant feather hat on her for a TV special, when the news came through that 'Can't Get You Out of My Head', had got to Number One. We were alone in her dressing room and both so excited we did a crazy little dance around the room!

CHRISTIAN LOUBOUTIN

Kylie and William make a great team because they are driven by two easy things – pleasure and efficiency – so whatever you have to do for Kylie is never that complicated. One of my favourite fashion moments was her wearing a thigh-high blue and gold pair of boots of mine, which made her look like a cross between a circus horse rider, a pop princess and a music-hall fairy.

KYLIE

I can't tell you how often people are staring at my feet...well, my shoes! As a shoe lover, I had a wonderful day at Louboutin's studio in Paris where his craftsmen took my measurements and made a last for me. Mine would be added to the countless others, each pair with a fabulous and recognizable name attributed to it. His creations are astounding and have many a time completed my look for a shoot or performance.

WILLIAM

The gold sequin dress was from Jean Paul Gaultier's 'Hollywood Couture' show and was featured in a segment based upon *Sunset Boulevard*.

KYLIE

This dress was exquisite. With its mass of tiny degrade sequins, it was as if it was dripping from the shoulders, and it just oozed glamour.

WILLIAM

Aphrodite, the goddess of love and desire, was born from the ocean waves. I wanted to create the ambience of Mykonos in a studio, so we built a white temple-like structure a long way from the glaring heat of the Aegean. Azure mirrors and black sand brought our island fantasy to life. With the 'Aphrodite' album's rich sounds of joyful pop and dance music, I wanted to celebrate love and to present Kylie as the goddess of love and desire herself. The blue dress by Gaultier Paris was perfect to bring the goddess to life, its swathes of blue chiffon billowing in the breeze – not of the Aegean winds unfortunately, but of an oversized wind machine.

KYLIE

The 'Aphrodite' dress could not have been more perfect. It was taken from Jean Paul's couture show and was worn by one of the smallest models, so it was as if it was made for me. Usually a costume or outfit has to be sourced or made, but sometimes serendipity comes into play and what I need just appears! It was meant to be.

overleaf left

LEANNE BUCKHAM

Snapped backstage five minutes after the red carpet in Cannes. To me this captures the spirit of off-duty Kylie.

KYLIE

With so many posed or staged photos, I need to release a bit of madness, and Leanne often captures that moment, the 'other' side of me; the one who has finished work and can finally let go.

overleaf right

KYLIE

I loved the Balmain collection from 2007, especially a feather print T-shirt which sadly came a-cropper in the wash. Yes, disaster. From a beautiful pale pink to a colour I can only call dirge! His next collection was all about strong looks, sexy military and shoulders! I had a fitting with Christophe Decarnin in Paris and wore plenty of his little mini dresses.

KYLIE

This creation by Jean Paul Gaultier was just perfect.
It had the grace and loveliness which was the
sentiment of the song, but it gave the imagery an
edge. It's a look that many fans recreate to wear to
my concerts. It's fantastic when a look can translate
into something achievable by everyone at home.
The boots were by the amazing Pierre Hardy.
We had to customize them, as they were about
four sizes too big, and then change them to white.

WILLIAM

How these photos came out at all is a miracle, as we were all so hungover that Kylie was positively green and I couldn't steady the camera, so we kept having to be fed burgers between shots by Kylie's PA, Leanne. Thus the shots are all sat down! Kylie was doing her own hair and make-up and could barely focus to draw on her eyeliner, let alone stick on individual lashes.

KYLIE

The Hotel George V in Paris is stunning. My friend Jeff Leatham creates all the flower installations there and provided the flowers for this shoot. The famous bar in the lobby created a drink in my honour called a 'Pink Pearl'. It's not only delicious, but dangerous, and I think we had one too many the night before this shoot. Coincidentally Willie arrived hungover from London, so the shoot was not our easiest, but we got through it. I tried to hide my face or sit down for as many shots as possible! The dark and sexy Yves Saint Laurent clothing worked for us and I ended up very pleased with the shoot.

GILES DEACON FOR UNGARO

below

The black-and-white lace dress was made while I was designing for Emanuel Ungaro. It was made entirely by the couture atelier and consisted of lace de Calais, with some incredible Lesage embroidered sea urchins on it. We also made a mascot sheep called Fungaro. I really liked the couture, sexy playfulness complimented by Fungaro the sheep. He got to go on tour to South America as well. Genius and hysterical!

opposite

JULIEN MACDONALD

Kylie has constantly been an inspiration to me. It has been wonderful to watch her grow and to witness her fashion style evolve. She knows what she wants, and when we work together she always wants more, more, more sparkles! She really is the Queen of Sparkle and even named me Mr Crystal. She is glamorous, sophisticated and full of fun.

KYLIE

I wore Julien's floaty creation for a TV performance in Mexico. I was excited to wear it as it was light, with lots of chiffon floating down the back.

overleaf

VICKY GILL

Creating a dress for the launch of Kylie's 'Aphrodite' album was such a treat I could have burst with excitement. My aim was to combine 'Performance Glamour' with a 'Grecian Goddess' twist. This dress is all about the 'Sparkle'. Twenty thousand Swarovski crystals took around seven days to cover a nude tulle base cut to compliment Kylie's perfect petite frame.

KYLIE

I adore this dress. Its simplicity and dreaminess allow the fantasy and emotion of the photo to shine through.

above

THE BLONDS

Working with Kylie is electrifying and what designer dreams are made of. William and Kylie have no boundaries, especially where glamour is concerned: everything is possible. This gown is hand-draped in fine silk jersey, featuring a crystal-encrusted corset with golden chain detail and cuffs. It was inspired by Kylie's 'Aphrodite' album and the story of Andromeda.

KYLIE

This incredible outfit felt and looked powerful. It fully came to life with the movement of a performance.

above & right

STEPHEN JONES

It's a great adventure working with Kylie. What is really unique about her is that we really create something together, not like a normal client relationship. She has so much experience I really learn from her, too, and together we make something beautiful. But one has to remember scale. Kylie is very petite so everything has to be perfectly proportioned. However, like Tinker Bell, she makes my hats come alive with a special sort of magic.

JULIAN BROAD

We shot these pictures in Milan at Dolce & Gabbana HQ. Fitting day for Kylie for the costumes for her upcoming 'Aphrodite Les Folies' tour... I've worked with Stefano and Domenico for many years, but this was my first time working with Kylie and she was a diamond – super pro and good fun. I guess they had a lot of tweaks to get through with the costumes, but all was done with charm and great humour. Stefano and Domenico clearly adore her. It was great seeing them, sleeves rolled up, getting really involved in adjusting the costumes, practising their craft. You don't get to see that every day. It was a pleasure to work with Kylie. Great girl; great arse!

WILLIAM

What is great about Dolce & Gabbana is how hands-on they are. They literally create in front of your eyes, snipping away, draping fabric here and there, and before you know it you're faced with an exquisite creation. For the 'Aphrodite Les Folies' tour a lot of the looks were inspired by styles and fashions they had explored and produced over their own twenty-year history. We wanted to reference the pure glamour and over-the-top couture of the 1930s and '40s Hollywood Folies extravaganzas, with inspirations ranging from Fellini's *Satyricon* and Rita Hayworth's *Salome* to Esther Williams's watery escapades brought to life by Busby Berkeley.

below & overleaf

DOLCE & GABBANA

In the 'Aphrodite' costumes, Kylie truly looked like a goddess.

WILLIAM

This show was perhaps the most succinct expression of fantasy and spectacle that we have produced. A gleaming white celestial temple on stage based on the architecture of classical Greece, with fountains pouring water and Kylie rising from the dry ice in an oversized golden shell, riding a golden pegasus or flying across the audience on an angel's back. The show was steeped in mythology and Hollywood glamour, and was a true pop odyssey. Dolce & Gabbana's costumes fitted perfectly into this otherworldly setting. Metres of chiffon and dripping gold laced their outfits, bringing Kylie as Aphrodite to life, a perfect fusion of fashion and fantasy, the ultimate sartorial expression of a pop goddess.

KYLIE

Fittings for a tour are long and can be difficult.
You're making decisions that you will need to stick
with for six months on the road; designs that need
to work for the audience in the front rows and up in
the 'gods'. We try everything: bodices, dresses, hats,
shoes and accessories. I was very proud when Stefano
and Domenico came to see their designs come to
life in the 'Aphrodite Les Folies' concert in their
hometown, Milano.

above & opposite

DOLCE & GABBANA

Kylie is beautiful and sexy, and she definitely knows how to play with fashion!

STEVIE STEWART

I collaborate with Will on the tours. For 'Aphrodite', I loved the challenge of designing and getting made a multitude of costumes, from huge articulated wings, shiny gold armour, saddlery and feather burlesque fans to corsetry, Brazilian carnival backpacks and Hollywood pompom couture gowns – not to mention the usual crystals and Lycra!

WILLIAM

Kylie feels most at home on stage, and for me the most fulfilling times we have had have been creating her elaborate stage shows. They are the most indulgent part of her fashion history and they are where she shines. Styling, directing and photographing Kylie is simply an indulgent exercise in fantasy, bringing our collective dreams alive.

overleaf

KYLIE

The special energy in Ibiza is undeniable. I love any opportunity to spend time on the island, and this shoot with Vincent Peters for Spanish *Vogue* didn't really feel like work. The sun was shining, the mood was great and the Dolce & Gabbana lingerie was perfect.

GILES DEACON

The dress we made here was the second in a series
we called 'Disco Fringe'. The colour of the hand-dyed
electric blue fringing looked fantastically chic, and then
as soon as there was dancing it was transformed into
a spinning, fringing disco ball of fun. The top of the
dress was embroidered with Swarovski crystal hologram
squares. It worked brilliantly as a stage piece, especially
on Kylie, who is tons of fun and classy – a rare, winning
combination! It is always fun, creative and exciting to
work with her and William.

KYLIE

I first met Giles through Katie Grand back in the day.
I wore his fringe mini dresses in various colours for
performances. His evening gowns are just stunning,
and he continues to create beautiful fashion. On top
of all that he is just the sweetest.

previous pages

MARK FAST

Working with such an influential artist as Kylie is a dream. She's so positive, and her music lifts the spirit of the nation. She's like a fairy godmother – always there when you need her. In fact, she's the perfect 'Fast woman'. Effortlessly beautiful... I love the image of the yellow and orange dress because it expresses the liberation of Kylie and my work in the same shot! Moments like this are why people are drawn to Kylie. As for the white crystal dress, if anyone could pull off this look, it would be her. She's like an exotic bird. She can work any dress I make and create the charisma I want to evoke. She's an inspiration, as she's a symbol of confidence and real beauty for men and women.

KYLIE

Mark's dresses can usually fit into a tiny bag. They are all about stretch, body con, sexy glamour. I wore the white crystalled dress to the Billboard Music Awards held in Las Vegas. The back is super-revealing but I figured I was just presenting an award and the back wouldn't really be seen. When I was waiting backstage to go on, the floor manager showed me where I had to walk and it was to a satellite stage that jutted out into the audience. From there I had to face the stage and present the award. Aaaahhhh!! So I took a deep breath in and hoped all would be OK. Thankfully, it was!

opposite & above

DAVID KOMA

I found the energy and creativity of working with Kylie and William a unique experience. Their way of working is so organic. Kylie makes whatever she tries on work, and adds a magical twist to each look. The 'Get Outta My Way' video was such a special moment for me... to see her wearing my dress in the opening scene. Kylie has always been a great inspiration for me, and her sense of style is incredible.

KYLIE

David makes dresses that can do the work for you. They are quite intricate designs and very inventive, but always conscious of the female form. The last fitting I did with him was in my kitchen. There were clothes absolutely everywhere, as he pinned and adjusted.

DOLCE & GABBANA

We've been working together for such a long time...we are friends. We are so proud that we have been able to dress Kylie throughout her artistic career, and we hope to continue doing so for many years to come. For us it's always a pleasure to create something special for our little princess.

opposite
PETER DUNDAS
FOR EMILIO PUCCI

Beyond the fact that Kylie is an iconic pop star, she's also one of the nicest people in show business. You're inspired and challenged to find the best in yourself because you know as a showman she does the same. Plus she has one of the best behinds in the business, so she's perfect in my clothes! Dressing Kylie is always great. I think everyone who works with her falls a little bit in love with her. I certainly did.

KYLIE MINOGUE

I remember each and every one of the photos in this book being taken. They all have a story and stir so many memories: the location, the travel, the drama, the laughs, tears and sometimes pain, the delight, the creativity, the circumstances, the result, the reaction. All this and so much more.

Fashion has been a permanent and continually evolving aspect of my career. It has afforded me a means of expression that no words or music can. Its power is a singular force and a mighty addition to the other elements of my career.

From rah-rah skirts to haute couture, it has been a wonderful journey. I understood early on that I was not one of those people who have the quality, which I admire, of having one clear and distinct style. My style is very much at the mercy of my mercurial nature and chameleon ways. How I feel like dressing one day is not necessarily how I will feel the next. On top of that, my fashion choices are dependent on the situation for which they are required: album cover, red carpet, tour spectacle, fashion editorial, royal engagement...

Touring costumes become like close friends, as we both work so hard every night performing. When the tour finishes and I see all the wear and tear of the costumes – blood, sweat, tears and triumph – the evidence of a shared experience is tangible. The intangible, naturally, goes much, much further. And I would need another (big) book to elaborate on all that.

I dislike being boxed into anything in all aspects of life. And so it is with clothes. When fashion feels like a freedom, I'm in love. But sartorial liberty isn't always the case, and often there is a price to pay. I have to find the balance between the majesty of a showgirl costume and how much it impedes my ability to move, to breathe, to perform (yes, there have been many panic attacks and even a couple of fainting spells getting out of some of the costumes seen in this book).

I've come a long way from cutting patterns with Nain, my grandmother, and making clothes as a teenager. It really is a dream to have worked so closely with some of the most inspiring and revolutionary designers of my time – collaborations of creativity and minds that will stay with me forever. And then there are all the other people who have helped make these dreams a reality: management, friends, stylists, set designers, hair and make-up artists, production companies, assistants and photographers. Way too many to mention, but they are all part of this story, and for that I am truly grateful.

Finally, some encounters have been fleeting, others longer lived, but each one in its own way has helped shape my definition of style. I look forward to many more fashion adventures, and most of all to sharing them with you.

Love always,

PICTURE CREDITS

INDEX

ACKNOWLEDGMENTS

Our thanks to everyone who has played a part in Kylie's fashion story. To her first stylists at Mushroom Records and then the Hit Factory, PWL. To Nicole Bonython, David Thomas, Judy Blame and Katie Grand, with whom the process of refining and experimentation has continued.

Thanks to all the photographers whose stunning imagery and endless creativity have captured Kylie for all eternity – especially Simon Emmett, Simon Fowler, Katerina Jebb, Lee Jenkins, Mert and Marcus, Xevi Muntané, Vincent Peters, Rankin, Stéphane Sednaoui and Ellen von Unwerth, but also countless others.

Thanks to all the video directors, particularly Dawn Shadforth, and the graphic designers, including Mark Farrow and Tony Hung, who have participated in making Kylie the visual pop artist she is today.

A huge thank you to all the fashion designers and fashion houses that have played a more than considerable part in Kylie's fashion legend and through whose collaborations she has produced some of her most enduring and interesting imagery: Balenciaga, Chanel, Dolce & Gabbana, John Galliano, Jean Paul Gaultier, Emilio Pucci, and many more; to London's vital and talented posse, including Antonio Berardi, Giles Deacon, Mark Fast, Owen Gaster, David Koma, Julien Macdonald, Meadham Kirchhoff, Mrs Jones, Richard Nicoll, Gareth Pugh and Stephen Jones.

Thanks to the shoe designers, including Manolo Blahnik, Jimmy Choo, Pierre Hardy, Jonathan Kelsey, Nicholas Kirkwood, Christian Louboutin and Giuseppe Zanotti.

Thanks to the unsung heroes who work away from the glare of the spotlight: the PRs, the stylist assistants, particularly Lucy Manning, Frank Strachan and Francesca Burns, and the hair and make-up artists Karen Alder, Caroline Barnes, Danilo, Malcolm Edwards, Alice Ghendri, Guido, Kabuki, Cyril Lalou, Sam McKnight, Johnnie Sapong, Eugene Souleiman and Christian Vermaark, to name but a few.

Thanks to the fashion magazines who have championed Kylie, and to the fans and music and fashion lovers who have followed her evolution of style.

Special thanks to Jelka Music, Alexis Roche, Salvo Nicosia, Alli Main, Yvonne Savage, Charlie Fenn and Natalie Stevenson, and to William Baker's photographic team led by Jenan Pekusic at ProVision Studios London.

Finally, extra special thanks to Julia Brukner, the champion of this book, and to Leanne Buckham, Georgie Baker and Terry Blamey.

First published in the United Kingdom in 2012 by Thames & Hudson Ltd, 181A High Holborn, London WC1V 7QX

Kylie / Fashion © 2012 Darenote Limited

All textual quotations © 2012 the individual contributors and Darenote Limited

All images save where otherwise indicated © 2012 Darenote Limited

www.kylie.com

British Library Cataloguing-in-Publication Data
A catalogue record for this book is available from the British Library

ISBN 978-0-500-51665-2

Printed and bound in China through Asia Pacific Offset Ltd.

To find out about all our publications, please visit **www.thamesandhudson.com**. There you can subscribe to our e-newsletter, browse or download our current catalogue, and buy any titles that are in print.

p. 1 Kylie in Gareth Pugh, photographed by William Baker.
p. 2 Kylie in Christopher Kane, photographed by William Baker.
pp. 4–5 Kylie in Balenciaga by Nicolas Ghesquière, photographed by Mert and Marcus.
p. 7 Kylie in Gaultier Paris, photographed by William Baker.
p. 8 Kylie in Dolce & Gabbana, photographed by William Baker.
p. 221 Kylie in David Koma and Dolce & Gabbana, with Giuseppe Zanotti boots, photographed by Christie Goodwin.